This book belongs to:

_____

 _____

Please email me if you find this notebook

index

index

index

100 books everyone should read before they die

1. "To Kill a Mockingbird" by Harper Lee
2. "Pride and Prejudice" by Jane Austen
3. "The Diary of Anne Frank" by Anne Frank
4. "1984" by George Orwell
5. Harry Potter and the Sorcerer's Stone" by J.K. Rowling
6. "The Lord of the Rings" (1-3) by J.R.R. Tolkien
7. "The Great Gatsby" by F. Scott Fitzgerald
8. "Charlotte's Web" by E.B. White
9. "The Hobbit" by J.R.R. Tolkien
10. "Little Women" by Louisa May Alcott
11. "Fahrenheit 451" by Ray Bradbury
12. "Jane Eyre" by Charlotte Bronte
13. "Animal Farm" by George Orwell
14. "Gone with the Wind" by Margaret Mitchell
15. "The Catcher in the Rye" by J.D. Salinger
16. "The Book Thief" by Markus Zusak
17. "The Adventures of Huckleberry Finn" by Mark Twain
18. "The Hunger Games" by Suzanne Collins
19. "The Help" by Kathryn Stockett
20. "The Lion, the Witch, and the Wadrobe" by C.S. Lewis
21. "The Grapes of Wrath" by John Steinbeck
22. "The Lord of the Flies" by William Golding
23. "The Kite Runner" by Khaled Hosseini
24. "Night" by Elie Wiesel
25. "Hamlet" by William Shakespeare
26. "A Wrinkle in Time" by Madeleine L'Engle
27. "Of Mice and Men" by John Steinbeck
28. "A Tale of Two Cities" by Charles Dickens
29. "Romeo and Juliet" by William Shakespeare
30. "The Hitchhikers Guide to the Galaxy" by Douglas Adams
31. "The Secret Garden" by Frances Hodgson Burnett
32. "A Christmas Carol" by Charles Dickens
33. "The Little Prince" by Antoine de Saint-Exupéry
34. "Brave New World" by Aldous Huxley
35. "Harry Potter and the Deathly Hallows" by J.K. Rowling
36. "The Giver" by Lois Lowry
37. "The Handmaid's Tale" by Margaret Atwood
38. "Where the Sidewalk Ends" by Shel Silverstein
39. "Wuthering Heights" Emily Bronte
40. "The Fault in Our Stars" by John Green
41. "Anne of Green Gables" by L.M. Montgomery
42. "The Adventures of Tom Sawyer" by Mark Twain
43. "Macbeth" by William Shakespeare
44. "The Girl with a Dragon Tattoo" by Stieg Larrson
45. "Frankenstein" by Mary Shelley
46. "The Holy Bible: King James Version"
47. "The Color Purple" by Alice Walker
48. "The Count of Monte Cristo" by Alexandre Dumas
49. "A Tree Grows in Brooklyn" by Betty Smith
50. "East of Eden" by John Steinbeck
51. "Alice in Wonderland" by Lewis Carroll
52. "In Cold Blood" by Truman Capote
53. "Catch-22" by Joseph Heller
54. "The Stand" by Stephen King
55. "Outlander" by Diana Gabaldon
56. "Harry Potter and the Prisoner of Azkaban" by J.K. Rowling
57. "Enders Game" by Orson Scott Card
58. "Anna Karenina" by Leo Tolstoy
59. "Watership Down" by Richard Adams
60. "Memoirs of a Geisha" by Arthur Golden
61. "Rebecca" by Daphne du Maurier
62. "A Game of Thrones" by George R.R. Martin
63. "Great Expectations" by Charles Dickens
64. "The Old Man and the Sea" by Ernest Hemingway
65. "The Adventures of Sherlock Holmes" (#3) by Arthur Conan Doyle
66. "Les Misérables" by Victor Hugo
67. "Harry Potter and the Half-Blood Prince" by J.K. Rowling
68. "Life of Pi" by Yann Martel
69. "The Scarlet Letter" by Nathaniel Hawthorne
70. "Celebrating Silence: Excerpts from Five Years of Weekly Knowledge" by Sri Sri Ravi Shankar
71. "The Chronicles of Narnia" by C.S. Lewis
72. "The Pillars of the Earth" by Ken Follett
73. "Catching Fire" by Suzanne Collins
74. "Charlie and the Chocolate Factory" by Roald Dahl
75. "Dracula" by Bram Stoker
76. "The Princess Bride" by William Goldman
77. "Water for Elephants" by Sara Gruen
78. "The Raven" by Edgar Allan Poe
79. "The Secret Life of Bees" by Sue Monk Kidd
80. "The Poisonwood Bible: A Novel" by Barbara Kingsolver
81. "One Hundred Years of Solitude" by Gabriel García Márquez
82. "The Time Traveler's Wife" by Audrey Niffenegger
83. "The Odyssey" by Homer
84. "The Good Earth (House of Earth #1)" by Pearl S. Buck
85. "Mockingjay (Hunger Games #3)" by Suzanne Collins
86. "And Then There Were None" by Agatha Christie
87. "The Thorn Birds" by Colleen McCullough
88. "A Prayer for Owen Meany" by John Irving
89. "The Glass Castle" by Jeannette Walls
90. "The Immortal Life of Henrietta Lacks" by Rebecca Skloot
91. "Crime and Punishment" by Fyodor Dostoyevsky
92. "The Road" by Cormac McCarthy
93. "The Things They Carried" by Tim O'Brien
94. "Siddhartha" by Hermann Hesse
95. "Beloved" by Toni Morrison
96. "Slaughterhouse-Five" by Kurt Vonnegut
97. "Cutting For Stone" by Abraham Verghese
98. "The Phantom Tollbooth" by Norton Juster
99. "The Brothers Karamazov" by Fyodor Dostoyevsky
100. "The Story of My Life" by Helen Keller

book wishlist

	Title	Author
☐		
☐		
☐		
☐		
☐		
☐		
☐		
☐		
☐		
☐		
☐		
☐		
☐		
☐		
☐		
☐		
☐		
☐		
☐		
☐		
☐		
☐		
☐		
☐		
☐		
☐		

book wishlist

	Title	Author
☐		
☐		
☐		
☐		
☐		
☐		
☐		
☐		
☐		
☐		
☐		
☐		
☐		
☐		
☐		
☐		
☐		
☐		
☐		
☐		
☐		
☐		
☐		
☐		

book wishlist

	Title	Author
☐		
☐		
☐		
☐		
☐		
☐		
☐		
☐		
☐		
☐		
☐		
☐		
☐		
☐		
☐		
☐		
☐		
☐		
☐		
☐		
☐		
☐		
☐		
☐		
☐		
☐		

book wishlist

	Title	Author
☐		
☐		
☐		
☐		
☐		
☐		
☐		
☐		
☐		
☐		
☐		
☐		
☐		
☐		
☐		
☐		
☐		
☐		
☐		
☐		
☐		
☐		
☐		
☐		
☐		
☐		

where are my books

Title	Borrower	Date borrowed	Date back

where are my books

Title	Borrower	Date borrowed	Date back

where are my books

Title	Borrower	Date borrowed	Date back

where are my books

Title	Borrower	Date borrowed	Date back

my favorite quotes

"

Book _____ Author_____ p_____

"

Book _____ Author_____ p_____

"

Book _____ Author_____ p_____

"

Book _____ Author_____ p_____

"

Book _____ Author_____ p_____

"

Book _____ Author_____ p_____

my favorite quotes

"

Book _____ Author_____ p_____

"

Book _____ Author_____ p_____

"

Book _____ Author_____ p_____

"

Book _____ Author_____ p_____

"

Book _____ Author_____ p_____

"

Book _____ Author_____ p_____

my favorite quotes

Quick list

"

Book _____ Author_____ p_____

"

Book _____ Author_____ p_____

"

Book _____ Author_____ p_____

"

Book _____ Author_____ p_____

"

Book _____ Author_____ p_____

"

Book _____ Author_____ p_____

my favorite quotes
Quick list

"

Book _____ Author_____ p_____

"

Book _____ Author_____ p_____

"

Book _____ Author_____ p_____

"

Book _____ Author_____ p_____

"

Book _____ Author_____ p_____

"

Book _____ Author_____ p_____

book review

Rating: ☆ ☆ ☆ ☆ ☆

Title _____

Author _____

Length
(pages/time) _____   Year
                                 published _____

Price _____   Recommended by _____

☐ Paper book ☐ e-book ☐ Audiobook ☐ Other _____

Started date	Finished date

FICTION

- ○ Action and adventure
- ○ Alternate history
- ○ Anthology
- ○ Chick lit
- ○ Children's
- ○ Comic book
- ○ Coming-of-age
- ○ Crime
- ○ Drama

- ○ Fairytale
- ○ Fantasy
- ○ Graphic novel
- ○ Historical fiction
- ○ Horror
- ○ Mystery
- ○ Paranormal romance
- ○ Picture book
- ○ Poetry

- ○ Political thriller
- ○ Romance
- ○ Satire
- ○ Science fiction
- ○ Short story
- ○ Suspense
- ○ Thriller
- ○ Young adult

NON-FICTION

- ○ Art
- ○ Autobiography
- ○ Biography
- ○ Cookbook
- ○ Diary
- ○ Dictionary
- ○ Encyclopedia
- ○ Guide

- ○ Health
- ○ History
- ○ Journal
- ○ Math
- ○ Memoir
- ○ Prayer
- ○ Religion, spirituality, and new age

- ○ Textbook
- ○ Review
- ○ Reference
- ○ Science
- ○ Self help
- ○ Travel
- ○ True crime

summary

my review

my favorite quote

book review

Rating: ☆ ☆ ☆ ☆ ☆

Title _____

Author _____

Length
(pages/time) _____

Year
published _____

Price _____   Recommended by _____

☐ Paper book ☐ e-book ☐ Audiobook ☐ Other _____

Started date	Finished date

FICTION

- ○ Action and adventure
- ○ Alternate history
- ○ Anthology
- ○ Chick lit
- ○ Children's
- ○ Comic book
- ○ Coming-of-age
- ○ Crime
- ○ Drama

- ○ Fairytale
- ○ Fantasy
- ○ Graphic novel
- ○ Historical fiction
- ○ Horror
- ○ Mystery
- ○ Paranormal romance
- ○ Picture book
- ○ Poetry

- ○ Political thriller
- ○ Romance
- ○ Satire
- ○ Science fiction
- ○ Short story
- ○ Suspense
- ○ Thriller
- ○ Young adult

NON-FICTION

- ○ Art
- ○ Autobiography
- ○ Biography
- ○ Cookbook
- ○ Diary
- ○ Dictionary
- ○ Encyclopedia
- ○ Guide

- ○ Health
- ○ History
- ○ Journal
- ○ Math
- ○ Memoir
- ○ Prayer
- ○ Religion, spirituality, and new age

- ○ Textbook
- ○ Review
- ○ Reference
- ○ Science
- ○ Self help
- ○ Travel
- ○ True crime

summary

my review

my favorite quote

book review

Rating: ☆ ☆ ☆ ☆ ☆

Title _____

Author _____

Length
(pages/time) _____

Year
published _____

Price _____

Recommended by _____

☐ Paper book ☐ e-book ☐ Audiobook ☐ Other _____

Started date

Finished date

FICTION

- O Action and adventure
- O Alternate history
- O Anthology
- O Chick lit
- O Children's
- O Comic book
- O Coming-of-age
- O Crime
- O Drama

- O Fairytale
- O Fantasy
- O Graphic novel
- O Historical fiction
- O Horror
- O Mystery
- O Paranormal romance
- O Picture book
- O Poetry

- O Political thriller
- O Romance
- O Satire
- O Science fiction
- O Short story
- O Suspense
- O Thriller
- O Young adult

NON-FICTION

- O Art
- O Autobiography
- O Biography
- O Cookbook
- O Diary
- O Dictionary
- O Encyclopedia
- O Guide

- O Health
- O History
- O Journal
- O Math
- O Memoir
- O Prayer
- O Religion, spirituality, and new age

- O Textbook
- O Review
- O Reference
- O Science
- O Self help
- O Travel
- O True crime

summary

my review

my favorite quote

book review

Rating: ☆ ☆ ☆ ☆ ☆

Title _____

Author _____

Length
(pages/time) _____

Year
published _____

Price _____

Recommended by _____

☐ Paper book ☐ e-book ☐ Audiobook ☐ Other _____

Started date	Finished date

FICTION

- ○ Action and adventure
- ○ Alternate history
- ○ Anthology
- ○ Chick lit
- ○ Children's
- ○ Comic book
- ○ Coming-of-age
- ○ Crime
- ○ Drama

- ○ Fairytale
- ○ Fantasy
- ○ Graphic novel
- ○ Historical fiction
- ○ Horror
- ○ Mystery
- ○ Paranormal romance
- ○ Picture book
- ○ Poetry

- ○ Political thriller
- ○ Romance
- ○ Satire
- ○ Science fiction
- ○ Short story
- ○ Suspense
- ○ Thriller
- ○ Young adult

NON-FICTION

- ○ Art
- ○ Autobiography
- ○ Biography
- ○ Cookbook
- ○ Diary
- ○ Dictionary
- ○ Encyclopedia
- ○ Guide

- ○ Health
- ○ History
- ○ Journal
- ○ Math
- ○ Memoir
- ○ Prayer
- ○ Religion, spirituality, and new age

- ○ Textbook
- ○ Review
- ○ Reference
- ○ Science
- ○ Self help
- ○ Travel
- ○ True crime

summary

my review

my favorite quote

book review

Rating: ☆ ☆ ☆ ☆ ☆

Title _____

Author _____

Length
(pages/time) _____   Year
published _____

Price _____   Recommended by _____

☐ Paper book ☐ e-book ☐ Audiobook ☐ Other _____

Started date	Finished date

FICTION

- Action and adventure
- Alternate history
- Anthology
- Chick lit
- Children's
- Comic book
- Coming-of-age
- Crime
- Drama

- Fairytale
- Fantasy
- Graphic novel
- Historical fiction
- Horror
- Mystery
- Paranormal romance
- Picture book
- Poetry

- Political thriller
- Romance
- Satire
- Science fiction
- Short story
- Suspense
- Thriller
- Young adult

NON-FICTION

- Art
- Autobiography
- Biography
- Cookbook
- Diary
- Dictionary
- Encyclopedia
- Guide

- Health
- History
- Journal
- Math
- Memoir
- Prayer
- Religion, spirituality, and new age

- Textbook
- Review
- Reference
- Science
- Self help
- Travel
- True crime

summary

my review

my favorite quote

"

"

book review

Rating: ☆ ☆ ☆ ☆ ☆

Title _____

Author _____

Length
(pages/time) _____

Year
published _____

Price _____   Recommended by _____

☐ Paper book ☐ e-book ☐ Audiobook ☐ Other _____

Started date	Finished date

FICTION

- ○ Action and adventure
- ○ Alternate history
- ○ Anthology
- ○ Chick lit
- ○ Children's
- ○ Comic book
- ○ Coming-of-age
- ○ Crime
- ○ Drama

- ○ Fairytale
- ○ Fantasy
- ○ Graphic novel
- ○ Historical fiction
- ○ Horror
- ○ Mystery
- ○ Paranormal romance
- ○ Picture book
- ○ Poetry

- ○ Political thriller
- ○ Romance
- ○ Satire
- ○ Science fiction
- ○ Short story
- ○ Suspense
- ○ Thriller
- ○ Young adult

NON-FICTION

- ○ Art
- ○ Autobiography
- ○ Biography
- ○ Cookbook
- ○ Diary
- ○ Dictionary
- ○ Encyclopedia
- ○ Guide

- ○ Health
- ○ History
- ○ Journal
- ○ Math
- ○ Memoir
- ○ Prayer
- ○ Religion, spirituality, and new age

- ○ Textbook
- ○ Review
- ○ Reference
- ○ Science
- ○ Self help
- ○ Travel
- ○ True crime

summary

my review

my favorite quote

book review

Rating: ☆ ☆ ☆ ☆ ☆

Title _____

Author _____

Length
(pages/time) _____   Year
published _____

Price _____   Recommended by _____

☐ Paper book ☐ e-book ☐ Audiobook ☐ Other _____

Started date	Finished date

FICTION

- ○ Action and adventure
- ○ Alternate history
- ○ Anthology
- ○ Chick lit
- ○ Children's
- ○ Comic book
- ○ Coming-of-age
- ○ Crime
- ○ Drama

- ○ Fairytale
- ○ Fantasy
- ○ Graphic novel
- ○ Historical fiction
- ○ Horror
- ○ Mystery
- ○ Paranormal romance
- ○ Picture book
- ○ Poetry

- ○ Political thriller
- ○ Romance
- ○ Satire
- ○ Science fiction
- ○ Short story
- ○ Suspense
- ○ Thriller
- ○ Young adult

NON-FICTION

- ○ Art
- ○ Autobiography
- ○ Biography
- ○ Cookbook
- ○ Diary
- ○ Dictionary
- ○ Encyclopedia
- ○ Guide

- ○ Health
- ○ History
- ○ Journal
- ○ Math
- ○ Memoir
- ○ Prayer
- ○ Religion, spirituality,
  and new age

- ○ Textbook
- ○ Review
- ○ Reference
- ○ Science
- ○ Self help
- ○ Travel
- ○ True crime

summary

my review

my favorite quote

book review

Rating: ☆ ☆ ☆ ☆ ☆

Title _____

Author _____

Length
(pages/time) _____

Year
published _____

Price _____

Recommended by _____

☐ Paper book ☐ e-book ☐ Audiobook ☐ Other _____

Started date	Finished date

FICTION

- ○ Action and adventure
- ○ Alternate history
- ○ Anthology
- ○ Chick lit
- ○ Children's
- ○ Comic book
- ○ Coming-of-age
- ○ Crime
- ○ Drama

- ○ Fairytale
- ○ Fantasy
- ○ Graphic novel
- ○ Historical fiction
- ○ Horror
- ○ Mystery
- ○ Paranormal romance
- ○ Picture book
- ○ Poetry

- ○ Political thriller
- ○ Romance
- ○ Satire
- ○ Science fiction
- ○ Short story
- ○ Suspense
- ○ Thriller
- ○ Young adult

NON-FICTION

- ○ Art
- ○ Autobiography
- ○ Biography
- ○ Cookbook
- ○ Diary
- ○ Dictionary
- ○ Encyclopedia
- ○ Guide

- ○ Health
- ○ History
- ○ Journal
- ○ Math
- ○ Memoir
- ○ Prayer
- ○ Religion, spirituality, and new age

- ○ Textbook
- ○ Review
- ○ Reference
- ○ Science
- ○ Self help
- ○ Travel
- ○ True crime

summary

my review

my favorite quote

book review

Rating: ☆ ☆ ☆ ☆ ☆

Title _____

Author _____

Length
(pages/time) _____   Year
                         published _____

Price _____   Recommended by _____

☐ Paper book ☐ e-book ☐ Audiobook ☐ Other _____

Started date	Finished date

FICTION

- ○ Action and adventure
- ○ Alternate history
- ○ Anthology
- ○ Chick lit
- ○ Children's
- ○ Comic book
- ○ Coming-of-age
- ○ Crime
- ○ Drama

- ○ Fairytale
- ○ Fantasy
- ○ Graphic novel
- ○ Historical fiction
- ○ Horror
- ○ Mystery
- ○ Paranormal romance
- ○ Picture book
- ○ Poetry

- ○ Political thriller
- ○ Romance
- ○ Satire
- ○ Science fiction
- ○ Short story
- ○ Suspense
- ○ Thriller
- ○ Young adult

NON-FICTION

- ○ Art
- ○ Autobiography
- ○ Biography
- ○ Cookbook
- ○ Diary
- ○ Dictionary
- ○ Encyclopedia
- ○ Guide

- ○ Health
- ○ History
- ○ Journal
- ○ Math
- ○ Memoir
- ○ Prayer
- ○ Religion, spirituality, and new age

- ○ Textbook
- ○ Review
- ○ Reference
- ○ Science
- ○ Self help
- ○ Travel
- ○ True crime

summary

my review

my favorite quote

book review

Rating: ☆ ☆ ☆ ☆ ☆

Title _____

Author _____

Length
(pages/time) _____   Year
published _____

Price _____   Recommended by _____

☐ Paper book ☐ e-book ☐ Audiobook ☐ Other _____

Started date	Finished date

FICTION

- ○ Action and adventure
- ○ Alternate history
- ○ Anthology
- ○ Chick lit
- ○ Children's
- ○ Comic book
- ○ Coming-of-age
- ○ Crime
- ○ Drama

- ○ Fairytale
- ○ Fantasy
- ○ Graphic novel
- ○ Historical fiction
- ○ Horror
- ○ Mystery
- ○ Paranormal romance
- ○ Picture book
- ○ Poetry

- ○ Political thriller
- ○ Romance
- ○ Satire
- ○ Science fiction
- ○ Short story
- ○ Suspense
- ○ Thriller
- ○ Young adult

NON-FICTION

- ○ Art
- ○ Autobiography
- ○ Biography
- ○ Cookbook
- ○ Diary
- ○ Dictionary
- ○ Encyclopedia
- ○ Guide

- ○ Health
- ○ History
- ○ Journal
- ○ Math
- ○ Memoir
- ○ Prayer
- ○ Religion, spirituality, and new age

- ○ Textbook
- ○ Review
- ○ Reference
- ○ Science
- ○ Self help
- ○ Travel
- ○ True crime

summary

my review

my favorite quote

book review

Rating: ☆ ☆ ☆ ☆ ☆

Title _____

Author _____

Length
(pages/time) _____

Year
published _____

Price _____

Recommended by _____

☐ Paper book ☐ e-book ☐ Audiobook ☐ Other _____

Started date	Finished date

FICTION

- ○ Action and adventure
- ○ Alternate history
- ○ Anthology
- ○ Chick lit
- ○ Children's
- ○ Comic book
- ○ Coming-of-age
- ○ Crime
- ○ Drama

- ○ Fairytale
- ○ Fantasy
- ○ Graphic novel
- ○ Historical fiction
- ○ Horror
- ○ Mystery
- ○ Paranormal romance
- ○ Picture book
- ○ Poetry

- ○ Political thriller
- ○ Romance
- ○ Satire
- ○ Science fiction
- ○ Short story
- ○ Suspense
- ○ Thriller
- ○ Young adult

NON-FICTION

- ○ Art
- ○ Autobiography
- ○ Biography
- ○ Cookbook
- ○ Diary
- ○ Dictionary
- ○ Encyclopedia
- ○ Guide

- ○ Health
- ○ History
- ○ Journal
- ○ Math
- ○ Memoir
- ○ Prayer
- ○ Religion, spirituality, and new age

- ○ Textbook
- ○ Review
- ○ Reference
- ○ Science
- ○ Self help
- ○ Travel
- ○ True crime

summary

my review

my favorite quote

book review

Rating: ☆ ☆ ☆ ☆ ☆

Title _____

Author _____

Length
(pages/time) _____   Year
published _____

Price _____   Recommended by _____

☐ Paper book ☐ e-book ☐ Audiobook ☐ Other _____

Started date	Finished date

FICTION

- ○ Action and adventure
- ○ Alternate history
- ○ Anthology
- ○ Chick lit
- ○ Children's
- ○ Comic book
- ○ Coming-of-age
- ○ Crime
- ○ Drama

- ○ Fairytale
- ○ Fantasy
- ○ Graphic novel
- ○ Historical fiction
- ○ Horror
- ○ Mystery
- ○ Paranormal romance
- ○ Picture book
- ○ Poetry

- ○ Political thriller
- ○ Romance
- ○ Satire
- ○ Science fiction
- ○ Short story
- ○ Suspense
- ○ Thriller
- ○ Young adult

NON-FICTION

- ○ Art
- ○ Autobiography
- ○ Biography
- ○ Cookbook
- ○ Diary
- ○ Dictionary
- ○ Encyclopedia
- ○ Guide

- ○ Health
- ○ History
- ○ Journal
- ○ Math
- ○ Memoir
- ○ Prayer
- ○ Religion, spirituality, and new age

- ○ Textbook
- ○ Review
- ○ Reference
- ○ Science
- ○ Self help
- ○ Travel
- ○ True crime

summary

my review

my favorite quote

book review

Rating: ☆ ☆ ☆ ☆ ☆

Title _____

Author _____

Length
(pages/time) _____

Year
published _____

Price _____

Recommended by _____

☐ Paper book ☐ e-book ☐ Audiobook ☐ Other _____

Started date	Finished date

FICTION

- ○ Action and adventure
- ○ Alternate history
- ○ Anthology
- ○ Chick lit
- ○ Children's
- ○ Comic book
- ○ Coming-of-age
- ○ Crime
- ○ Drama

- ○ Fairytale
- ○ Fantasy
- ○ Graphic novel
- ○ Historical fiction
- ○ Horror
- ○ Mystery
- ○ Paranormal romance
- ○ Picture book
- ○ Poetry

- ○ Political thriller
- ○ Romance
- ○ Satire
- ○ Science fiction
- ○ Short story
- ○ Suspense
- ○ Thriller
- ○ Young adult

NON-FICTION

- ○ Art
- ○ Autobiography
- ○ Biography
- ○ Cookbook
- ○ Diary
- ○ Dictionary
- ○ Encyclopedia
- ○ Guide

- ○ Health
- ○ History
- ○ Journal
- ○ Math
- ○ Memoir
- ○ Prayer
- ○ Religion, spirituality, and new age

- ○ Textbook
- ○ Review
- ○ Reference
- ○ Science
- ○ Self help
- ○ Travel
- ○ True crime

summary

my review

my favorite quote

book review

Rating: ☆ ☆ ☆ ☆ ☆

Title _____

Author _____

Length
(pages/time) _____

Year
published _____

Price _____

Recommended by _____

☐ Paper book ☐ e-book ☐ Audiobook ☐ Other _____

Started date	Finished date

FICTION

- ○ Action and adventure
- ○ Alternate history
- ○ Anthology
- ○ Chick lit
- ○ Children's
- ○ Comic book
- ○ Coming-of-age
- ○ Crime
- ○ Drama

- ○ Fairytale
- ○ Fantasy
- ○ Graphic novel
- ○ Historical fiction
- ○ Horror
- ○ Mystery
- ○ Paranormal romance
- ○ Picture book
- ○ Poetry

- ○ Political thriller
- ○ Romance
- ○ Satire
- ○ Science fiction
- ○ Short story
- ○ Suspense
- ○ Thriller
- ○ Young adult

NON-FICTION

- ○ Art
- ○ Autobiography
- ○ Biography
- ○ Cookbook
- ○ Diary
- ○ Dictionary
- ○ Encyclopedia
- ○ Guide

- ○ Health
- ○ History
- ○ Journal
- ○ Math
- ○ Memoir
- ○ Prayer
- ○ Religion, spirituality, and new age

- ○ Textbook
- ○ Review
- ○ Reference
- ○ Science
- ○ Self help
- ○ Travel
- ○ True crime

summary

my review

my favorite quote

book review

Rating: ☆ ☆ ☆ ☆ ☆

Title _____

Author _____

Length
(pages/time) _____   Year
published _____

Price _____   Recommended by _____

☐ Paper book ☐ e-book ☐ Audiobook ☐ Other _____

Started date	Finished date

FICTION
- ○ Action and adventure
- ○ Alternate history
- ○ Anthology
- ○ Chick lit
- ○ Children's
- ○ Comic book
- ○ Coming-of-age
- ○ Crime
- ○ Drama
- ○ Fairytale
- ○ Fantasy
- ○ Graphic novel
- ○ Historical fiction
- ○ Horror
- ○ Mystery
- ○ Paranormal romance
- ○ Picture book
- ○ Poetry
- ○ Political thriller
- ○ Romance
- ○ Satire
- ○ Science fiction
- ○ Short story
- ○ Suspense
- ○ Thriller
- ○ Young adult

NON-FICTION
- ○ Art
- ○ Autobiography
- ○ Biography
- ○ Cookbook
- ○ Diary
- ○ Dictionary
- ○ Encyclopedia
- ○ Guide
- ○ Health
- ○ History
- ○ Journal
- ○ Math
- ○ Memoir
- ○ Prayer
- ○ Religion, spirituality, and new age
- ○ Textbook
- ○ Review
- ○ Reference
- ○ Science
- ○ Self help
- ○ Travel
- ○ True crime

summary

my review

my favorite quote

book review

Rating: ☆ ☆ ☆ ☆ ☆

Title _____

Author _____

Length
(pages/time) _____   Year
                                published _____

Price _____   Recommended by _____

☐ Paper book ☐ e-book ☐ Audiobook ☐ Other _____

Started date	Finished date

FICTION

- ○ Action and adventure
- ○ Alternate history
- ○ Anthology
- ○ Chick lit
- ○ Children's
- ○ Comic book
- ○ Coming-of-age
- ○ Crime
- ○ Drama

- ○ Fairytale
- ○ Fantasy
- ○ Graphic novel
- ○ Historical fiction
- ○ Horror
- ○ Mystery
- ○ Paranormal romance
- ○ Picture book
- ○ Poetry

- ○ Political thriller
- ○ Romance
- ○ Satire
- ○ Science fiction
- ○ Short story
- ○ Suspense
- ○ Thriller
- ○ Young adult

NON-FICTION

- ○ Art
- ○ Autobiography
- ○ Biography
- ○ Cookbook
- ○ Diary
- ○ Dictionary
- ○ Encyclopedia
- ○ Guide

- ○ Health
- ○ History
- ○ Journal
- ○ Math
- ○ Memoir
- ○ Prayer
- ○ Religion, spirituality, and new age

- ○ Textbook
- ○ Review
- ○ Reference
- ○ Science
- ○ Self help
- ○ Travel
- ○ True crime

summary

my review

my favorite quote

book review

Rating: ☆ ☆ ☆ ☆ ☆

Title _____

Author _____

Length
(pages/time) _____

Year
published _____

Price _____

Recommended by _____

☐ Paper book ☐ e-book ☐ Audiobook ☐ Other _____

Started date

Finished date

FICTION

- ○ Action and adventure
- ○ Alternate history
- ○ Anthology
- ○ Chick lit
- ○ Children's
- ○ Comic book
- ○ Coming-of-age
- ○ Crime
- ○ Drama

- ○ Fairytale
- ○ Fantasy
- ○ Graphic novel
- ○ Historical fiction
- ○ Horror
- ○ Mystery
- ○ Paranormal romance
- ○ Picture book
- ○ Poetry

- ○ Political thriller
- ○ Romance
- ○ Satire
- ○ Science fiction
- ○ Short story
- ○ Suspense
- ○ Thriller
- ○ Young adult

NON-FICTION

- ○ Art
- ○ Autobiography
- ○ Biography
- ○ Cookbook
- ○ Diary
- ○ Dictionary
- ○ Encyclopedia
- ○ Guide

- ○ Health
- ○ History
- ○ Journal
- ○ Math
- ○ Memoir
- ○ Prayer
- ○ Religion, spirituality,
  and new age

- ○ Textbook
- ○ Review
- ○ Reference
- ○ Science
- ○ Self help
- ○ Travel
- ○ True crime

summary

my review

my favorite quote

book review

Rating: ☆ ☆ ☆ ☆ ☆

Title _____

Author _____

Length
(pages/time) _____   Year
published _____

Price _____   Recommended by _____

☐ Paper book ☐ e-book ☐ Audiobook ☐ Other _____

Started date	Finished date

FICTION

- ○ Action and adventure
- ○ Alternate history
- ○ Anthology
- ○ Chick lit
- ○ Children's
- ○ Comic book
- ○ Coming-of-age
- ○ Crime
- ○ Drama

- ○ Fairytale
- ○ Fantasy
- ○ Graphic novel
- ○ Historical fiction
- ○ Horror
- ○ Mystery
- ○ Paranormal romance
- ○ Picture book
- ○ Poetry

- ○ Political thriller
- ○ Romance
- ○ Satire
- ○ Science fiction
- ○ Short story
- ○ Suspense
- ○ Thriller
- ○ Young adult

NON-FICTION

- ○ Art
- ○ Autobiography
- ○ Biography
- ○ Cookbook
- ○ Diary
- ○ Dictionary
- ○ Encyclopedia
- ○ Guide

- ○ Health
- ○ History
- ○ Journal
- ○ Math
- ○ Memoir
- ○ Prayer
- ○ Religion, spirituality, and new age

- ○ Textbook
- ○ Review
- ○ Reference
- ○ Science
- ○ Self help
- ○ Travel
- ○ True crime

summary

my review

my favorite quote

book review

Rating: ☆ ☆ ☆ ☆ ☆

Title _____

Author _____

Length
(pages/time) _____   Year
published _____

Price _____   Recommended by _____

☐ Paper book ☐ e-book ☐ Audiobook ☐ Other _____

Started date	Finished date

FICTION

- ○ Action and adventure
- ○ Alternate history
- ○ Anthology
- ○ Chick lit
- ○ Children's
- ○ Comic book
- ○ Coming-of-age
- ○ Crime
- ○ Drama

- ○ Fairytale
- ○ Fantasy
- ○ Graphic novel
- ○ Historical fiction
- ○ Horror
- ○ Mystery
- ○ Paranormal romance
- ○ Picture book
- ○ Poetry

- ○ Political thriller
- ○ Romance
- ○ Satire
- ○ Science fiction
- ○ Short story
- ○ Suspense
- ○ Thriller
- ○ Young adult

NON-FICTION

- ○ Art
- ○ Autobiography
- ○ Biography
- ○ Cookbook
- ○ Diary
- ○ Dictionary
- ○ Encyclopedia
- ○ Guide

- ○ Health
- ○ History
- ○ Journal
- ○ Math
- ○ Memoir
- ○ Prayer
- ○ Religion, spirituality, and new age

- ○ Textbook
- ○ Review
- ○ Reference
- ○ Science
- ○ Self help
- ○ Travel
- ○ True crime

summary

my review

my favorite quote

book review

Rating: ☆ ☆ ☆ ☆ ☆

Title _____

Author _____

Length
(pages/time) _____   Year
published _____

Price _____   Recommended by _____

☐ Paper book ☐ e-book ☐ Audiobook ☐ Other _____

Started date	Finished date

FICTION

- ○ Action and adventure
- ○ Alternate history
- ○ Anthology
- ○ Chick lit
- ○ Children's
- ○ Comic book
- ○ Coming-of-age
- ○ Crime
- ○ Drama

- ○ Fairytale
- ○ Fantasy
- ○ Graphic novel
- ○ Historical fiction
- ○ Horror
- ○ Mystery
- ○ Paranormal romance
- ○ Picture book
- ○ Poetry

- ○ Political thriller
- ○ Romance
- ○ Satire
- ○ Science fiction
- ○ Short story
- ○ Suspense
- ○ Thriller
- ○ Young adult

NON-FICTION

- ○ Art
- ○ Autobiography
- ○ Biography
- ○ Cookbook
- ○ Diary
- ○ Dictionary
- ○ Encyclopedia
- ○ Guide

- ○ Health
- ○ History
- ○ Journal
- ○ Math
- ○ Memoir
- ○ Prayer
- ○ Religion, spirituality, and new age

- ○ Textbook
- ○ Review
- ○ Reference
- ○ Science
- ○ Self help
- ○ Travel
- ○ True crime

summary

my review

my favorite quote

"

"

book review

Rating: ☆ ☆ ☆ ☆ ☆

Title _____

Author _____

Length
(pages/time) _____

Year
published _____

Price _____

Recommended by _____

☐ Paper book ☐ e-book ☐ Audiobook ☐ Other _____

Started date	Finished date

FICTION

- ○ Action and adventure
- ○ Alternate history
- ○ Anthology
- ○ Chick lit
- ○ Children's
- ○ Comic book
- ○ Coming-of-age
- ○ Crime
- ○ Drama

- ○ Fairytale
- ○ Fantasy
- ○ Graphic novel
- ○ Historical fiction
- ○ Horror
- ○ Mystery
- ○ Paranormal romance
- ○ Picture book
- ○ Poetry

- ○ Political thriller
- ○ Romance
- ○ Satire
- ○ Science fiction
- ○ Short story
- ○ Suspense
- ○ Thriller
- ○ Young adult

NON-FICTION

- ○ Art
- ○ Autobiography
- ○ Biography
- ○ Cookbook
- ○ Diary
- ○ Dictionary
- ○ Encyclopedia
- ○ Guide

- ○ Health
- ○ History
- ○ Journal
- ○ Math
- ○ Memoir
- ○ Prayer
- ○ Religion, spirituality, and new age

- ○ Textbook
- ○ Review
- ○ Reference
- ○ Science
- ○ Self help
- ○ Travel
- ○ True crime

summary

my review

my favorite quote

book review

Rating: ☆ ☆ ☆ ☆ ☆

Title	_____
Author	_____

Length (pages/time)	_____	Year published	_____
Price	_____	Recommended by	_____

☐ Paper book ☐ e-book ☐ Audiobook ☐ Other _____

Started date

Finished date

FICTION

- ○ Action and adventure
- ○ Alternate history
- ○ Anthology
- ○ Chick lit
- ○ Children's
- ○ Comic book
- ○ Coming-of-age
- ○ Crime
- ○ Drama

- ○ Fairytale
- ○ Fantasy
- ○ Graphic novel
- ○ Historical fiction
- ○ Horror
- ○ Mystery
- ○ Paranormal romance
- ○ Picture book
- ○ Poetry

- ○ Political thriller
- ○ Romance
- ○ Satire
- ○ Science fiction
- ○ Short story
- ○ Suspense
- ○ Thriller
- ○ Young adult

NON-FICTION

- ○ Art
- ○ Autobiography
- ○ Biography
- ○ Cookbook
- ○ Diary
- ○ Dictionary
- ○ Encyclopedia
- ○ Guide

- ○ Health
- ○ History
- ○ Journal
- ○ Math
- ○ Memoir
- ○ Prayer
- ○ Religion, spirituality, and new age

- ○ Textbook
- ○ Review
- ○ Reference
- ○ Science
- ○ Self help
- ○ Travel
- ○ True crime

summary

my review

my favorite quote

book review

Rating: ☆ ☆ ☆ ☆ ☆

Title _____

Author _____

Length
(pages/time) _____   Year
published _____

Price _____   Recommended by _____

☐ Paper book ☐ e-book ☐ Audiobook ☐ Other _____

Started date	Finished date

FICTION

- O Action and adventure
- O Alternate history
- O Anthology
- O Chick lit
- O Children's
- O Comic book
- O Coming-of-age
- O Crime
- O Drama

- O Fairytale
- O Fantasy
- O Graphic novel
- O Historical fiction
- O Horror
- O Mystery
- O Paranormal romance
- O Picture book
- O Poetry

- O Political thriller
- O Romance
- O Satire
- O Science fiction
- O Short story
- O Suspense
- O Thriller
- O Young adult

NON-FICTION

- O Art
- O Autobiography
- O Biography
- O Cookbook
- O Diary
- O Dictionary
- O Encyclopedia
- O Guide

- O Health
- O History
- O Journal
- O Math
- O Memoir
- O Prayer
- O Religion, spirituality, and new age

- O Textbook
- O Review
- O Reference
- O Science
- O Self help
- O Travel
- O True crime

summary

my review

my favorite quote

book review

Rating: ☆ ☆ ☆ ☆ ☆

Title _____

Author _____

Length
(pages/time) _____

Year
published _____

Price _____

Recommended by _____

☐ Paper book ☐ e-book ☐ Audiobook ☐ Other _____

Started date	Finished date

FICTION

- O Action and adventure
- O Alternate history
- O Anthology
- O Chick lit
- O Children's
- O Comic book
- O Coming-of-age
- O Crime
- O Drama

- O Fairytale
- O Fantasy
- O Graphic novel
- O Historical fiction
- O Horror
- O Mystery
- O Paranormal romance
- O Picture book
- O Poetry

- O Political thriller
- O Romance
- O Satire
- O Science fiction
- O Short story
- O Suspense
- O Thriller
- O Young adult

NON-FICTION

- O Art
- O Autobiography
- O Biography
- O Cookbook
- O Diary
- O Dictionary
- O Encyclopedia
- O Guide

- O Health
- O History
- O Journal
- O Math
- O Memoir
- O Prayer
- O Religion, spirituality, and new age

- O Textbook
- O Review
- O Reference
- O Science
- O Self help
- O Travel
- O True crime

summary

my review

my favorite quote

book review

Rating: ☆ ☆ ☆ ☆ ☆

Title _____

Author _____

Length
(pages/time) _____

Year
published _____

Price _____

Recommended by _____

☐ Paper book ☐ e-book ☐ Audiobook ☐ Other _____

Started date	Finished date

FICTION
- O Action and adventure
- O Alternate history
- O Anthology
- O Chick lit
- O Children's
- O Comic book
- O Coming-of-age
- O Crime
- O Drama

- O Fairytale
- O Fantasy
- O Graphic novel
- O Historical fiction
- O Horror
- O Mystery
- O Paranormal romance
- O Picture book
- O Poetry

- O Political thriller
- O Romance
- O Satire
- O Science fiction
- O Short story
- O Suspense
- O Thriller
- O Young adult

NON-FICTION
- O Art
- O Autobiography
- O Biography
- O Cookbook
- O Diary
- O Dictionary
- O Encyclopedia
- O Guide

- O Health
- O History
- O Journal
- O Math
- O Memoir
- O Prayer
- O Religion, spirituality, and new age

- O Textbook
- O Review
- O Reference
- O Science
- O Self help
- O Travel
- O True crime

summary

my review

my favorite quote

"

"

book review

Rating: ☆ ☆ ☆ ☆ ☆

Title _____

Author _____

Length
(pages/time) _____

Year
published _____

Price _____

Recommended by _____

☐ Paper book ☐ e-book ☐ Audiobook ☐ Other _____

Started date

Finished date

FICTION

- ○ Action and adventure
- ○ Alternate history
- ○ Anthology
- ○ Chick lit
- ○ Children's
- ○ Comic book
- ○ Coming-of-age
- ○ Crime
- ○ Drama

- ○ Fairytale
- ○ Fantasy
- ○ Graphic novel
- ○ Historical fiction
- ○ Horror
- ○ Mystery
- ○ Paranormal romance
- ○ Picture book
- ○ Poetry

- ○ Political thriller
- ○ Romance
- ○ Satire
- ○ Science fiction
- ○ Short story
- ○ Suspense
- ○ Thriller
- ○ Young adult

NON-FICTION

- ○ Art
- ○ Autobiography
- ○ Biography
- ○ Cookbook
- ○ Diary
- ○ Dictionary
- ○ Encyclopedia
- ○ Guide

- ○ Health
- ○ History
- ○ Journal
- ○ Math
- ○ Memoir
- ○ Prayer
- ○ Religion, spirituality, and new age

- ○ Textbook
- ○ Review
- ○ Reference
- ○ Science
- ○ Self help
- ○ Travel
- ○ True crime

summary

my review

my favorite quote

book review

Rating: ☆ ☆ ☆ ☆ ☆

Title _____

Author _____

Length
(pages/time) _____

Year
published _____

Price _____

Recommended by _____

☐ Paper book ☐ e-book ☐ Audiobook ☐ Other _____

Started date	Finished date

FICTION

- O Action and adventure
- O Alternate history
- O Anthology
- O Chick lit
- O Children's
- O Comic book
- O Coming-of-age
- O Crime
- O Drama

- O Fairytale
- O Fantasy
- O Graphic novel
- O Historical fiction
- O Horror
- O Mystery
- O Paranormal romance
- O Picture book
- O Poetry

- O Political thriller
- O Romance
- O Satire
- O Science fiction
- O Short story
- O Suspense
- O Thriller
- O Young adult

NON-FICTION

- O Art
- O Autobiography
- O Biography
- O Cookbook
- O Diary
- O Dictionary
- O Encyclopedia
- O Guide

- O Health
- O History
- O Journal
- O Math
- O Memoir
- O Prayer
- O Religion, spirituality, and new age

- O Textbook
- O Review
- O Reference
- O Science
- O Self help
- O Travel
- O True crime

summary

my review

my favorite quote

book review

Rating: ☆ ☆ ☆ ☆ ☆

Title _____

Author _____

Length
(pages/time) _____   Year
published _____

Price _____   Recommended by _____

☐ Paper book ☐ e-book ☐ Audiobook ☐ Other _____

Started date	Finished date

FICTION

- ○ Action and adventure
- ○ Alternate history
- ○ Anthology
- ○ Chick lit
- ○ Children's
- ○ Comic book
- ○ Coming-of-age
- ○ Crime
- ○ Drama

- ○ Fairytale
- ○ Fantasy
- ○ Graphic novel
- ○ Historical fiction
- ○ Horror
- ○ Mystery
- ○ Paranormal romance
- ○ Picture book
- ○ Poetry

- ○ Political thriller
- ○ Romance
- ○ Satire
- ○ Science fiction
- ○ Short story
- ○ Suspense
- ○ Thriller
- ○ Young adult

NON-FICTION

- ○ Art
- ○ Autobiography
- ○ Biography
- ○ Cookbook
- ○ Diary
- ○ Dictionary
- ○ Encyclopedia
- ○ Guide

- ○ Health
- ○ History
- ○ Journal
- ○ Math
- ○ Memoir
- ○ Prayer
- ○ Religion, spirituality, and new age

- ○ Textbook
- ○ Review
- ○ Reference
- ○ Science
- ○ Self help
- ○ Travel
- ○ True crime

summary

my review

my favorite quote

book review

Rating: ☆ ☆ ☆ ☆ ☆

Title _____

Author _____

Length
(pages/time) _____   Year
                                published _____

Price _____   Recommended by _____

☐ Paper book ☐ e-book ☐ Audiobook ☐ Other _____

Started date	Finished date

FICTION

- O Action and adventure
- O Alternate history
- O Anthology
- O Chick lit
- O Children's
- O Comic book
- O Coming-of-age
- O Crime
- O Drama

- O Fairytale
- O Fantasy
- O Graphic novel
- O Historical fiction
- O Horror
- O Mystery
- O Paranormal romance
- O Picture book
- O Poetry

- O Political thriller
- O Romance
- O Satire
- O Science fiction
- O Short story
- O Suspense
- O Thriller
- O Young adult

NON-FICTION

- O Art
- O Autobiography
- O Biography
- O Cookbook
- O Diary
- O Dictionary
- O Encyclopedia
- O Guide

- O Health
- O History
- O Journal
- O Math
- O Memoir
- O Prayer
- O Religion, spirituality, and new age

- O Textbook
- O Review
- O Reference
- O Science
- O Self help
- O Travel
- O True crime

summary

my review

my favorite quote

"

"

book review

Rating: ☆ ☆ ☆ ☆ ☆

Title _____

Author _____

Length
(pages/time) _____

Year
published _____

Price _____

Recommended by _____

☐ Paper book ☐ e-book ☐ Audiobook ☐ Other _____

Started date	Finished date

FICTION

- O Action and adventure
- O Alternate history
- O Anthology
- O Chick lit
- O Children's
- O Comic book
- O Coming-of-age
- O Crime
- O Drama

- O Fairytale
- O Fantasy
- O Graphic novel
- O Historical fiction
- O Horror
- O Mystery
- O Paranormal romance
- O Picture book
- O Poetry

- O Political thriller
- O Romance
- O Satire
- O Science fiction
- O Short story
- O Suspense
- O Thriller
- O Young adult

NON-FICTION

- O Art
- O Autobiography
- O Biography
- O Cookbook
- O Diary
- O Dictionary
- O Encyclopedia
- O Guide

- O Health
- O History
- O Journal
- O Math
- O Memoir
- O Prayer
- O Religion, spirituality, and new age

- O Textbook
- O Review
- O Reference
- O Science
- O Self help
- O Travel
- O True crime

summary

my review

my favorite quote

book review

Rating: ☆ ☆ ☆ ☆ ☆

Title _____

Author _____

Length
(pages/time) _____

Year
published _____

Price _____

Recommended by _____

☐ Paper book ☐ e-book ☐ Audiobook ☐ Other _____

Started date

Finished date

FICTION

- ○ Action and adventure
- ○ Alternate history
- ○ Anthology
- ○ Chick lit
- ○ Children's
- ○ Comic book
- ○ Coming-of-age
- ○ Crime
- ○ Drama

- ○ Fairytale
- ○ Fantasy
- ○ Graphic novel
- ○ Historical fiction
- ○ Horror
- ○ Mystery
- ○ Paranormal romance
- ○ Picture book
- ○ Poetry

- ○ Political thriller
- ○ Romance
- ○ Satire
- ○ Science fiction
- ○ Short story
- ○ Suspense
- ○ Thriller
- ○ Young adult

NON-FICTION

- ○ Art
- ○ Autobiography
- ○ Biography
- ○ Cookbook
- ○ Diary
- ○ Dictionary
- ○ Encyclopedia
- ○ Guide

- ○ Health
- ○ History
- ○ Journal
- ○ Math
- ○ Memoir
- ○ Prayer
- ○ Religion, spirituality, and new age

- ○ Textbook
- ○ Review
- ○ Reference
- ○ Science
- ○ Self help
- ○ Travel
- ○ True crime

summary

my review

my favorite quote

" "

book review

Rating: ☆ ☆ ☆ ☆ ☆

Title _____

Author _____

Length
(pages/time) _____

Year
published _____

Price _____

Recommended by _____

☐ Paper book ☐ e-book ☐ Audiobook ☐ Other _____

Started date

Finished date

FICTION

- ○ Action and adventure
- ○ Alternate history
- ○ Anthology
- ○ Chick lit
- ○ Children's
- ○ Comic book
- ○ Coming-of-age
- ○ Crime
- ○ Drama

- ○ Fairytale
- ○ Fantasy
- ○ Graphic novel
- ○ Historical fiction
- ○ Horror
- ○ Mystery
- ○ Paranormal romance
- ○ Picture book
- ○ Poetry

- ○ Political thriller
- ○ Romance
- ○ Satire
- ○ Science fiction
- ○ Short story
- ○ Suspense
- ○ Thriller
- ○ Young adult

NON-FICTION

- ○ Art
- ○ Autobiography
- ○ Biography
- ○ Cookbook
- ○ Diary
- ○ Dictionary
- ○ Encyclopedia
- ○ Guide

- ○ Health
- ○ History
- ○ Journal
- ○ Math
- ○ Memoir
- ○ Prayer
- ○ Religion, spirituality, and new age

- ○ Textbook
- ○ Review
- ○ Reference
- ○ Science
- ○ Self help
- ○ Travel
- ○ True crime

summary

my review

my favorite quote

"

"

book review

Rating: ☆ ☆ ☆ ☆ ☆

Title _____

Author _____

Length
(pages/time) _____   Year
published _____

Price _____   Recommended by _____

☐ Paper book ☐ e-book ☐ Audiobook ☐ Other _____

Started date

Finished date

FICTION

- ○ Action and adventure
- ○ Alternate history
- ○ Anthology
- ○ Chick lit
- ○ Children's
- ○ Comic book
- ○ Coming-of-age
- ○ Crime
- ○ Drama

- ○ Fairytale
- ○ Fantasy
- ○ Graphic novel
- ○ Historical fiction
- ○ Horror
- ○ Mystery
- ○ Paranormal romance
- ○ Picture book
- ○ Poetry

- ○ Political thriller
- ○ Romance
- ○ Satire
- ○ Science fiction
- ○ Short story
- ○ Suspense
- ○ Thriller
- ○ Young adult

NON-FICTION

- ○ Art
- ○ Autobiography
- ○ Biography
- ○ Cookbook
- ○ Diary
- ○ Dictionary
- ○ Encyclopedia
- ○ Guide

- ○ Health
- ○ History
- ○ Journal
- ○ Math
- ○ Memoir
- ○ Prayer
- ○ Religion, spirituality, and new age

- ○ Textbook
- ○ Review
- ○ Reference
- ○ Science
- ○ Self help
- ○ Travel
- ○ True crime

summary

my review

my favorite quote

book review

Rating: ☆ ☆ ☆ ☆ ☆

Title _____

Author _____

Length
(pages/time) _____

Year
published _____

Price _____   Recommended by _____

☐ Paper book ☐ e-book ☐ Audiobook ☐ Other _____

Started date	Finished date

FICTION

- ○ Action and adventure
- ○ Alternate history
- ○ Anthology
- ○ Chick lit
- ○ Children's
- ○ Comic book
- ○ Coming-of-age
- ○ Crime
- ○ Drama

- ○ Fairytale
- ○ Fantasy
- ○ Graphic novel
- ○ Historical fiction
- ○ Horror
- ○ Mystery
- ○ Paranormal romance
- ○ Picture book
- ○ Poetry

- ○ Political thriller
- ○ Romance
- ○ Satire
- ○ Science fiction
- ○ Short story
- ○ Suspense
- ○ Thriller
- ○ Young adult

NON-FICTION

- ○ Art
- ○ Autobiography
- ○ Biography
- ○ Cookbook
- ○ Diary
- ○ Dictionary
- ○ Encyclopedia
- ○ Guide

- ○ Health
- ○ History
- ○ Journal
- ○ Math
- ○ Memoir
- ○ Prayer
- ○ Religion, spirituality, and new age

- ○ Textbook
- ○ Review
- ○ Reference
- ○ Science
- ○ Self help
- ○ Travel
- ○ True crime

summary

my review

my favorite quote

book review

Rating: ☆ ☆ ☆ ☆ ☆

Title _____

Author _____

Length
(pages/time) _____

Year
published _____

Price _____

Recommended by _____

☐ Paper book ☐ e-book ☐ Audiobook ☐ Other _____

Started date	Finished date

FICTION

- ○ Action and adventure
- ○ Alternate history
- ○ Anthology
- ○ Chick lit
- ○ Children's
- ○ Comic book
- ○ Coming-of-age
- ○ Crime
- ○ Drama
- ○ Fairytale
- ○ Fantasy
- ○ Graphic novel
- ○ Historical fiction
- ○ Horror
- ○ Mystery
- ○ Paranormal romance
- ○ Picture book
- ○ Poetry
- ○ Political thriller
- ○ Romance
- ○ Satire
- ○ Science fiction
- ○ Short story
- ○ Suspense
- ○ Thriller
- ○ Young adult

NON-FICTION

- ○ Art
- ○ Autobiography
- ○ Biography
- ○ Cookbook
- ○ Diary
- ○ Dictionary
- ○ Encyclopedia
- ○ Guide
- ○ Health
- ○ History
- ○ Journal
- ○ Math
- ○ Memoir
- ○ Prayer
- ○ Religion, spirituality, and new age
- ○ Textbook
- ○ Review
- ○ Reference
- ○ Science
- ○ Self help
- ○ Travel
- ○ True crime

summary

my review

my favorite quote

book review

Rating: ☆ ☆ ☆ ☆ ☆

Title _____

Author _____

Length
(pages/time) _____   Year published _____

Price _____   Recommended by _____

☐ Paper book ☐ e-book ☐ Audiobook ☐ Other _____

Started date

Finished date

FICTION

- ○ Action and adventure
- ○ Alternate history
- ○ Anthology
- ○ Chick lit
- ○ Children's
- ○ Comic book
- ○ Coming-of-age
- ○ Crime
- ○ Drama

- ○ Fairytale
- ○ Fantasy
- ○ Graphic novel
- ○ Historical fiction
- ○ Horror
- ○ Mystery
- ○ Paranormal romance
- ○ Picture book
- ○ Poetry

- ○ Political thriller
- ○ Romance
- ○ Satire
- ○ Science fiction
- ○ Short story
- ○ Suspense
- ○ Thriller
- ○ Young adult

NON-FICTION

- ○ Art
- ○ Autobiography
- ○ Biography
- ○ Cookbook
- ○ Diary
- ○ Dictionary
- ○ Encyclopedia
- ○ Guide

- ○ Health
- ○ History
- ○ Journal
- ○ Math
- ○ Memoir
- ○ Prayer
- ○ Religion, spirituality, and new age

- ○ Textbook
- ○ Review
- ○ Reference
- ○ Science
- ○ Self help
- ○ Travel
- ○ True crime

summary

my review

my favorite quote

book review

Rating: ☆ ☆ ☆ ☆ ☆

Title _____

Author _____

Length
(pages/time) _____   Year
published _____

Price _____   Recommended by _____

☐ Paper book ☐ e-book ☐ Audiobook ☐ Other _____

Started date

Finished date

FICTION
- ○ Action and adventure
- ○ Alternate history
- ○ Anthology
- ○ Chick lit
- ○ Children's
- ○ Comic book
- ○ Coming-of-age
- ○ Crime
- ○ Drama

- ○ Fairytale
- ○ Fantasy
- ○ Graphic novel
- ○ Historical fiction
- ○ Horror
- ○ Mystery
- ○ Paranormal romance
- ○ Picture book
- ○ Poetry

- ○ Political thriller
- ○ Romance
- ○ Satire
- ○ Science fiction
- ○ Short story
- ○ Suspense
- ○ Thriller
- ○ Young adult

NON-FICTION
- ○ Art
- ○ Autobiography
- ○ Biography
- ○ Cookbook
- ○ Diary
- ○ Dictionary
- ○ Encyclopedia
- ○ Guide

- ○ Health
- ○ History
- ○ Journal
- ○ Math
- ○ Memoir
- ○ Prayer
- ○ Religion, spirituality,
  and new age

- ○ Textbook
- ○ Review
- ○ Reference
- ○ Science
- ○ Self help
- ○ Travel
- ○ True crime

summary

my review

my favorite quote

book review

Rating: ☆ ☆ ☆ ☆ ☆

Title _____

Author _____

Length
(pages/time) _____   Year
published _____

Price _____   Recommended by _____

☐ Paper book ☐ e-book ☐ Audiobook ☐ Other _____

Started date	Finished date

FICTION

- ○ Action and adventure
- ○ Alternate history
- ○ Anthology
- ○ Chick lit
- ○ Children's
- ○ Comic book
- ○ Coming-of-age
- ○ Crime
- ○ Drama

- ○ Fairytale
- ○ Fantasy
- ○ Graphic novel
- ○ Historical fiction
- ○ Horror
- ○ Mystery
- ○ Paranormal romance
- ○ Picture book
- ○ Poetry

- ○ Political thriller
- ○ Romance
- ○ Satire
- ○ Science fiction
- ○ Short story
- ○ Suspense
- ○ Thriller
- ○ Young adult

NON-FICTION

- ○ Art
- ○ Autobiography
- ○ Biography
- ○ Cookbook
- ○ Diary
- ○ Dictionary
- ○ Encyclopedia
- ○ Guide

- ○ Health
- ○ History
- ○ Journal
- ○ Math
- ○ Memoir
- ○ Prayer
- ○ Religion, spirituality,
  and new age

- ○ Textbook
- ○ Review
- ○ Reference
- ○ Science
- ○ Self help
- ○ Travel
- ○ True crime

summary

my review

my favorite quote

book review

Rating: ☆ ☆ ☆ ☆ ☆

Title _____

Author _____

Length
(pages/time) _____   Year
                          published _____

Price _____   Recommended by _____

☐ Paper book ☐ e-book ☐ Audiobook ☐ Other _____

Started date	Finished date

FICTION

- ○ Action and adventure
- ○ Alternate history
- ○ Anthology
- ○ Chick lit
- ○ Children's
- ○ Comic book
- ○ Coming-of-age
- ○ Crime
- ○ Drama

- ○ Fairytale
- ○ Fantasy
- ○ Graphic novel
- ○ Historical fiction
- ○ Horror
- ○ Mystery
- ○ Paranormal romance
- ○ Picture book
- ○ Poetry

- ○ Political thriller
- ○ Romance
- ○ Satire
- ○ Science fiction
- ○ Short story
- ○ Suspense
- ○ Thriller
- ○ Young adult

NON-FICTION

- ○ Art
- ○ Autobiography
- ○ Biography
- ○ Cookbook
- ○ Diary
- ○ Dictionary
- ○ Encyclopedia
- ○ Guide

- ○ Health
- ○ History
- ○ Journal
- ○ Math
- ○ Memoir
- ○ Prayer
- ○ Religion, spirituality,
  and new age

- ○ Textbook
- ○ Review
- ○ Reference
- ○ Science
- ○ Self help
- ○ Travel
- ○ True crime

summary

my review

my favorite quote

book review

Rating: ☆ ☆ ☆ ☆ ☆

Title _____

Author _____

Length
(pages/time) _____

Year
published _____

Price _____

Recommended by _____

☐ Paper book ☐ e-book ☐ Audiobook ☐ Other _____

Started date

Finished date

FICTION

- ○ Action and adventure
- ○ Alternate history
- ○ Anthology
- ○ Chick lit
- ○ Children's
- ○ Comic book
- ○ Coming-of-age
- ○ Crime
- ○ Drama

- ○ Fairytale
- ○ Fantasy
- ○ Graphic novel
- ○ Historical fiction
- ○ Horror
- ○ Mystery
- ○ Paranormal romance
- ○ Picture book
- ○ Poetry

- ○ Political thriller
- ○ Romance
- ○ Satire
- ○ Science fiction
- ○ Short story
- ○ Suspense
- ○ Thriller
- ○ Young adult

NON-FICTION

- ○ Art
- ○ Autobiography
- ○ Biography
- ○ Cookbook
- ○ Diary
- ○ Dictionary
- ○ Encyclopedia
- ○ Guide

- ○ Health
- ○ History
- ○ Journal
- ○ Math
- ○ Memoir
- ○ Prayer
- ○ Religion, spirituality, and new age

- ○ Textbook
- ○ Review
- ○ Reference
- ○ Science
- ○ Self help
- ○ Travel
- ○ True crime

summary

my review

my favorite quote

"

"

book review

Rating: ☆ ☆ ☆ ☆ ☆

Title _____

Author _____

Length
(pages/time) _____

Year
published _____

Price _____

Recommended by _____

☐ Paper book ☐ e-book ☐ Audiobook ☐ Other _____

Started date	Finished date

FICTION

- O Action and adventure
- O Alternate history
- O Anthology
- O Chick lit
- O Children's
- O Comic book
- O Coming-of-age
- O Crime
- O Drama

- O Fairytale
- O Fantasy
- O Graphic novel
- O Historical fiction
- O Horror
- O Mystery
- O Paranormal romance
- O Picture book
- O Poetry

- O Political thriller
- O Romance
- O Satire
- O Science fiction
- O Short story
- O Suspense
- O Thriller
- O Young adult

NON-FICTION

- O Art
- O Autobiography
- O Biography
- O Cookbook
- O Diary
- O Dictionary
- O Encyclopedia
- O Guide

- O Health
- O History
- O Journal
- O Math
- O Memoir
- O Prayer
- O Religion, spirituality,
  and new age

- O Textbook
- O Review
- O Reference
- O Science
- O Self help
- O Travel
- O True crime

summary

my review

my favorite quote

book review

Rating: ☆ ☆ ☆ ☆ ☆

Title _____

Author _____

Length
(pages/time) _____

Year
published _____

Price _____

Recommended by _____

☐ Paper book ☐ e-book ☐ Audiobook ☐ Other _____

Started date	Finished date

FICTION

- O Action and adventure
- O Alternate history
- O Anthology
- O Chick lit
- O Children's
- O Comic book
- O Coming-of-age
- O Crime
- O Drama

- O Fairytale
- O Fantasy
- O Graphic novel
- O Historical fiction
- O Horror
- O Mystery
- O Paranormal romance
- O Picture book
- O Poetry

- O Political thriller
- O Romance
- O Satire
- O Science fiction
- O Short story
- O Suspense
- O Thriller
- O Young adult

NON-FICTION

- O Art
- O Autobiography
- O Biography
- O Cookbook
- O Diary
- O Dictionary
- O Encyclopedia
- O Guide

- O Health
- O History
- O Journal
- O Math
- O Memoir
- O Prayer
- O Religion, spirituality, and new age

- O Textbook
- O Review
- O Reference
- O Science
- O Self help
- O Travel
- O True crime

summary

my review

my favorite quote

book review

Rating: ☆ ☆ ☆ ☆ ☆

Title _____

Author _____

Length
(pages/time) _____   Year
published _____

Price _____   Recommended by _____

☐ Paper book ☐ e-book ☐ Audiobook ☐ Other _____

Started date	Finished date

FICTION

- ○ Action and adventure
- ○ Alternate history
- ○ Anthology
- ○ Chick lit
- ○ Children's
- ○ Comic book
- ○ Coming-of-age
- ○ Crime
- ○ Drama

- ○ Fairytale
- ○ Fantasy
- ○ Graphic novel
- ○ Historical fiction
- ○ Horror
- ○ Mystery
- ○ Paranormal romance
- ○ Picture book
- ○ Poetry

- ○ Political thriller
- ○ Romance
- ○ Satire
- ○ Science fiction
- ○ Short story
- ○ Suspense
- ○ Thriller
- ○ Young adult

NON-FICTION

- ○ Art
- ○ Autobiography
- ○ Biography
- ○ Cookbook
- ○ Diary
- ○ Dictionary
- ○ Encyclopedia
- ○ Guide

- ○ Health
- ○ History
- ○ Journal
- ○ Math
- ○ Memoir
- ○ Prayer
- ○ Religion, spirituality, and new age

- ○ Textbook
- ○ Review
- ○ Reference
- ○ Science
- ○ Self help
- ○ Travel
- ○ True crime

summary

my review

my favorite quote

book review

Rating: ☆ ☆ ☆ ☆ ☆

Title _____

Author _____

Length
(pages/time) _____   Year
published _____

Price _____   Recommended by _____

☐ Paper book ☐ e-book ☐ Audiobook ☐ Other _____

Started date	Finished date

FICTION

- ○ Action and adventure
- ○ Alternate history
- ○ Anthology
- ○ Chick lit
- ○ Children's
- ○ Comic book
- ○ Coming-of-age
- ○ Crime
- ○ Drama

- ○ Fairytale
- ○ Fantasy
- ○ Graphic novel
- ○ Historical fiction
- ○ Horror
- ○ Mystery
- ○ Paranormal romance
- ○ Picture book
- ○ Poetry

- ○ Political thriller
- ○ Romance
- ○ Satire
- ○ Science fiction
- ○ Short story
- ○ Suspense
- ○ Thriller
- ○ Young adult

NON-FICTION

- ○ Art
- ○ Autobiography
- ○ Biography
- ○ Cookbook
- ○ Diary
- ○ Dictionary
- ○ Encyclopedia
- ○ Guide

- ○ Health
- ○ History
- ○ Journal
- ○ Math
- ○ Memoir
- ○ Prayer
- ○ Religion, spirituality, and new age

- ○ Textbook
- ○ Review
- ○ Reference
- ○ Science
- ○ Self help
- ○ Travel
- ○ True crime

summary

my review

my favorite quote

book review

Rating: ☆ ☆ ☆ ☆ ☆

Title _____

Author _____

Length
(pages/time) _____

Year
published _____

Price _____

Recommended by _____

☐ Paper book ☐ e-book ☐ Audiobook ☐ Other _____

Started date	Finished date

FICTION

- ○ Action and adventure
- ○ Alternate history
- ○ Anthology
- ○ Chick lit
- ○ Children's
- ○ Comic book
- ○ Coming-of-age
- ○ Crime
- ○ Drama

- ○ Fairytale
- ○ Fantasy
- ○ Graphic novel
- ○ Historical fiction
- ○ Horror
- ○ Mystery
- ○ Paranormal romance
- ○ Picture book
- ○ Poetry

- ○ Political thriller
- ○ Romance
- ○ Satire
- ○ Science fiction
- ○ Short story
- ○ Suspense
- ○ Thriller
- ○ Young adult

NON-FICTION

- ○ Art
- ○ Autobiography
- ○ Biography
- ○ Cookbook
- ○ Diary
- ○ Dictionary
- ○ Encyclopedia
- ○ Guide

- ○ Health
- ○ History
- ○ Journal
- ○ Math
- ○ Memoir
- ○ Prayer
- ○ Religion, spirituality, and new age

- ○ Textbook
- ○ Review
- ○ Reference
- ○ Science
- ○ Self help
- ○ Travel
- ○ True crime

summary

my review

my favorite quote

book review

Rating: ☆☆☆☆☆

Title _____

Author _____

Length
(pages/time) _____

Year
published _____

Price _____

Recommended by _____

☐ Paper book ☐ e-book ☐ Audiobook ☐ Other _____

Started date

Finished date

FICTION

- ○ Action and adventure
- ○ Alternate history
- ○ Anthology
- ○ Chick lit
- ○ Children's
- ○ Comic book
- ○ Coming-of-age
- ○ Crime
- ○ Drama

- ○ Fairytale
- ○ Fantasy
- ○ Graphic novel
- ○ Historical fiction
- ○ Horror
- ○ Mystery
- ○ Paranormal romance
- ○ Picture book
- ○ Poetry

- ○ Political thriller
- ○ Romance
- ○ Satire
- ○ Science fiction
- ○ Short story
- ○ Suspense
- ○ Thriller
- ○ Young adult

NON-FICTION

- ○ Art
- ○ Autobiography
- ○ Biography
- ○ Cookbook
- ○ Diary
- ○ Dictionary
- ○ Encyclopedia
- ○ Guide

- ○ Health
- ○ History
- ○ Journal
- ○ Math
- ○ Memoir
- ○ Prayer
- ○ Religion, spirituality, and new age

- ○ Textbook
- ○ Review
- ○ Reference
- ○ Science
- ○ Self help
- ○ Travel
- ○ True crime

summary

my review

my favorite quote

book review

Rating: ☆ ☆ ☆ ☆ ☆

Title _____

Author _____

Length
(pages/time) _____

Year
published _____

Price _____

Recommended by _____

☐ Paper book ☐ e-book ☐ Audiobook ☐ Other _____

Started date	Finished date

FICTION

- O Action and adventure
- O Alternate history
- O Anthology
- O Chick lit
- O Children's
- O Comic book
- O Coming-of-age
- O Crime
- O Drama

- O Fairytale
- O Fantasy
- O Graphic novel
- O Historical fiction
- O Horror
- O Mystery
- O Paranormal romance
- O Picture book
- O Poetry

- O Political thriller
- O Romance
- O Satire
- O Science fiction
- O Short story
- O Suspense
- O Thriller
- O Young adult

NON-FICTION

- O Art
- O Autobiography
- O Biography
- O Cookbook
- O Diary
- O Dictionary
- O Encyclopedia
- O Guide

- O Health
- O History
- O Journal
- O Math
- O Memoir
- O Prayer
- O Religion, spirituality, and new age

- O Textbook
- O Review
- O Reference
- O Science
- O Self help
- O Travel
- O True crime

summary

my review

my favorite quote

"

"

book review

Rating: ☆ ☆ ☆ ☆ ☆

Title _____

Author _____

Length
(pages/time) _____

Year
published _____

Price _____

Recommended by _____

☐ Paper book ☐ e-book ☐ Audiobook ☐ Other _____

Started date

Finished date

FICTION

- ○ Action and adventure
- ○ Alternate history
- ○ Anthology
- ○ Chick lit
- ○ Children's
- ○ Comic book
- ○ Coming-of-age
- ○ Crime
- ○ Drama

- ○ Fairytale
- ○ Fantasy
- ○ Graphic novel
- ○ Historical fiction
- ○ Horror
- ○ Mystery
- ○ Paranormal romance
- ○ Picture book
- ○ Poetry

- ○ Political thriller
- ○ Romance
- ○ Satire
- ○ Science fiction
- ○ Short story
- ○ Suspense
- ○ Thriller
- ○ Young adult

NON-FICTION

- ○ Art
- ○ Autobiography
- ○ Biography
- ○ Cookbook
- ○ Diary
- ○ Dictionary
- ○ Encyclopedia
- ○ Guide

- ○ Health
- ○ History
- ○ Journal
- ○ Math
- ○ Memoir
- ○ Prayer
- ○ Religion, spirituality, and new age

- ○ Textbook
- ○ Review
- ○ Reference
- ○ Science
- ○ Self help
- ○ Travel
- ○ True crime

summary

my review

my favorite quote

"

"

Made in the USA
Monee, IL
26 March 2022

93605884R00070